I Can't Stop Worrying!

A holistic guide to help children cope with stress and anxiety

Story:
Arlene Curcio Armbrecht
Kelly McMahon Brown

Illustrations:
Adam C. Armbrecht

Layout & Design:
Adam C. Armbrecht

Concept Art:
Arlene Curcio Armbrecht

An important note: This book is not intended as a substitute for the medical recommendations of physicians or other healthcare providers. Rather it is intended to offer information to help adults and children cooperate with physicians and health professionals in a mutual quest for optimum well-being.

Copyright (c) 2015 by Two Healthy Chicks Publishing
First Trade Paperback Edition, 2015
All rights reserved. This book, or parts thereof, may not be reproduced in any form without permission.

ISBN - 13: 978-1517688660
ISBN -10: 1517688663

This book is dedicated to Dr. Sachiko Komagato. As our professor, our mentor and staunch advocate for holistic health, Dr. Kamagato inspired us to explore and share all avenues for health and wellness. She embodies the compassion and dedication that made studying under her a unique, powerful experience.

For this we are truly thankful.

Holistic health is a concept that incorporates the whole person using the connection of mind, body and spirit to help attain wellness and balance. For all those who work with, live with or just love children, this book is for you.

Its purpose is to give insight, strategies and holistic methods to help children cope with stress and anxiety. It is not intended to replace conventional methods or a doctor's advice, but rather as an adjunct for wellness and healing. Each child is unique. One technique may work more effectively for some, while another will work better for others. Practice makes perfect!

This is a diagram whose paths can be changed. Use it as a guide to learn easy and effective approaches. It is best to read through the "notes to adults" prior to sharing this story with your child. Again, this is meant to be read with love and laughter.

There is no right or wrong approach. Read it. Try it. Play with it. While we believe these techniques are highly effective, if after practicing several of the interventions in this book, your child's anxiety is not improving or becomes debilitating, it is advisable to speak with someone such as your family doctor, School Nurse, Student Assistance Counselor or School Psychologist who may refer you to a community health professional. The goal of this book is to begin a conversation and open up a world of possibilities.

Love and Health,

Arlene and Kelly

Notes to Adults:

You can't always judge a person by how they appear on the outside. Everyone, at one time or another, has a problem or issue that affects them emotionally on the inside.

My name is James....

and I look like
a regular boy on the outside....

Notes to Adults:

The symptoms that James is experiencing could be from anxiety. Anxiety is defined as apprehension or excessive fear about real or imagined circumstances. Feeling anxious is normal but when worry becomes excessive, a child's ability to function may become impaired.

Symptoms of anxiety may vary. Anxiety may start in your head, but can lead to problems throughout the body. Some children always feel tired or have trouble concentrating. Others may be easily startled or have problems falling or staying asleep. For some, stomach issues may occur because the gut is very sensitive to emotional stress.

But on the inside, I have butterflies in my stomach, my heart beats way too fast and my brain won't sleep because...

I CAN'T STOP WORRYING!

Notes to Adults:

It is natural for children to worry at times and due to personality and temperament, some may worry more than others. Sometimes we see the problems of children as small when we as adults are dealing with so much more. We need to remember that they are young and to them their problems seem quite monumental. It is important to acknowledge and respect their feelings and concerns. If your child seems worried about something, try to find out what is on their mind. Be available and take an interest in their world. Sometimes just having your attention or getting a nice hug can make them feel better.

My mom and dad keep asking me if SOMETHING is BOTHERING me.

The problem is A LOT of things bother me!

I worry about going on the school bus.
I worry about being smart enough.
I worry about being picked last for kickball.

I worry about what I will eat for lunch.
I worry about making friends.
I worry that I will get sick.
I worry that I will miss home.

I WORRY ABOUT EVERYTHING!!!!!!

Notes to Adults:

Anxiety can cause some children to feel frightened and distressed where others would not feel that way. Be aware of changes in your child's behavior. Make note of the amount of time he or she spends in worry mode.

Guiding your child to start the day off on a positive note is a crucial component. The next few pages will explain several methods to encourage and produce a confident foundation.

> Things to discuss:
>
> Can you tell me about a time when you were worried or anxious?
>
> What did that feel like?

One morning I woke up tired, my stomach hurt and I was shaking.

I tried to get out of bed but I felt frozen, like I was stuck in my favorite popsicle!
Mom came in and
this is what happened. . . .

Notes to Adults:

While experiencing anxiety, our breathing rate and pattern changes, becoming quick and shallow, which can sometimes lead to hyperventilation. Breathing exercises can help bring the nervous system back into balance causing a relaxation response.

> Breathing Technique:
>
> 1. Place a hand on your belly to help guide you in taking deep cleansing breaths. You should breathe in and out through your nose.
>
> 2. Take a deep breath while counting slowly to five. The belly should rise like an expanding balloon.
>
> 3. Exhale long and slow while counting to five.
>
> 4. An advanced technique would include pausing between inhalation and exhalation.

Mom pulled me into her lap, gave me a big hug and asked me what was wrong.
I told her "I'm not sure but... I can't stop worrying."

Mom told me she could help and I felt a little better. She told me to breathe in through my nose as she slowly counted to 5.

Then I breathed out the same way 5,4,3,2,1. I imagined hundreds of tiny bubbles floating all around me!

Suddenly, I felt warm and stopped shaking!

Notes to Adults:

Yoga is an energy medicine designed to put pressure on the endocrine system, releasing those happy, feel good hormones while squeezing stress and tension out of the body, much like wringing the water out of a wet washcloth. One need not be a Yogi Master to perform a few safe, simple poses. These may help alleviate anxiety and stress, soothe the mind, and signal the body and breath to slow down. No worries if the poses are not perfect... trying may even evoke some giggling and laughter! This too can be quite therapeutic!

Mountain Pose: Stand with your feet hip distance apart, tummy squeezed in. Relax your shoulders and press your feet into the floor, inhaling and exhaling deeply and slowly through the nose.

Forward Fold: From mountain pose, take a deep inhale raising your arms up overhead. On the exhale, fold forward, fingertips on the floor. Rest in this position, hanging like a rag doll for several deep breaths.

Downward Dog: From forward fold, go down to the floor on all fours like a table. Your hands should be under your shoulders and knees under your hips. Inhale through your nose and lift your hips toward the ceiling making an inverted "V" shape. Keep your eyes on your toes and press your heels toward the floor. Exhale deeply as you relax into the pose. Stay in this position for at least three long breaths.

Mom then showed me how to do some yoga!

We started with a position called Mountain Pose and ended with Downward Dog!

At first I didn't want to try it but I did. I giggled trying to get it just right!

I felt like a strong, tall giraffe, dangling its long neck!

Notes to Adults:

Anxiety in children can also be addressed through diet. Sometimes kids can be picky, but try to serve them as many clean foods as you can. This means foods that come from the earth without additives or preservatives. Eat colorfully. Avoid packaged foods as well as those empty calories from drinks or snacks loaded with sugar or caffeine. Drinking plenty of water is another important element.

What we eat can affect how we feel. Proper nutrition is crucial to feeling well and fueling the body.

> Things to Discuss:
>
> 1. What could you have for dinner tonight that has at least three colors? Example: chicken (yellow), broccoli (green), and sweet potato (orange).
>
> 2. What are some healthy snacks you can chose? Example: fresh fruit or veggies with yogurt or melted peanut butter or almond butter.

I got dressed and went downstairs.
Mom explained that to feel good you need
to eat breakfast to give you energy for the day!

I ate a banana and whole grain toast
with peanut butter.
What did you have for breakfast today??

Notes to Adults:

You are acknowledging your child's concerns, but trying to limit the amount of time spent ruminating on them. By having a special worry box or time, you can give your child the opportunity to let go for a bit. Put their worries in the box!

To create your own worry box:

1. Use any small container or box.

2. Decorate the box with colors or items special to your child. The decorations can be anything that interests your child, such as a beach or sports theme.

3. Putting a picture in the bottom of the box depicting nature, such as flowers or trees, underscores the importance of being outdoors with its therapeutic influence on health and wellness.

4. You can also put a special stone that holds their worries in the box or even a special drawing or poem.

After breakfast, mom brought me a little container she called my worry box.

"For now," she said, "put all your worries right in here."

Notes to Adults:

Focusing on the good things and being grateful allows our thoughts to bend toward the positive.

It is easy to get caught up in negative thinking.

Practicing Gratitude:

Encourage the child to talk about what they are grateful for.

You can prompt with words such as family, friends, pets, and toys.

Mom drove me to school that day and on the way we talked about my favorite things...

my puppy that likes to lick my face
and summertime
when I can go swimming in the lake!
What are some of your favorite things?

Notes to Adults:

Art:

Art is a visual language that helps get what is happening on the inside out. It can be extremely helpful when a child finds it hard to put what they feel into words. It's not about perfection but expression. Anyone can be an artist!

Essential Oils:

Using pure essential oils such as lavender or lemon balm help to relieve anxiety. These aromas affect a part of the brain that controls heart rate, blood pressure, breathing, memory, stress levels and hormone balance.

To use essential oils:

1. Mix 3 drops of oil in a small spray bottle of water. You can mist this in the air.

2. Put 3 drops of oil on a cotton ball which can be put in an open dish, or even a small container or plastic bag to carry with you.

3. Ready made sprays of essential oils are available in health food stores or easily found online.

At school mom introduced me to a really nice lady named Ms. Kitt, the Student Assistance Counselor. She told me that I could come to see her if I was worrying at school.

She gave me crayons and paper and told me to draw a picture of what was bothering me.

Her office smelled really good. Ms. Kitt told me it was Lavender.

Notes to Adults:

Guided imagery is a techinque in which a person can take a mental break from stress and anxiety and imagine being somwhere relaxing, fun and safe. One can be "guided" by a recording or another person, usually with soothing music in the background.

Children generally love guided imagery because it allows their imaginations to take them wherever they want to go. Visualization or guided imagery uses not only your visual sense, but also your sense of smell, taste, touch and sound. It helps free you of tension, and you can use any scene or situation that is pleasurable.

Things to Remember:

You can use any scenario that would engage the child. It could be a walk in the woods with rustling trees and chirping birds or dangling your toes in a cool babbling brook.

Remember to use each of the five senses in your imagery.

When I got back to the classroom, kids were being very silly and loud. My teacher said, "Take your seat.

Close your eyes and imagine you are walking on the beach. You see pretty shells and hear the ocean waves crashing. The sand tickles your toes and you taste the fresh, salty air.

The warm sun shines on your face. Do you feel it? You are calm and relaxed."

I had my eyes closed tight, thinking, *I taste the salt on my tongue! It would be funny if I was being sprinkled by a giant salt shaker!!*

Everyone was ready to begin the first lesson of the day.

Notes to Adults:

Being outside, literally with your feet in the grass, is so important.

Nature takes us far away from stresses and strains and stimulates our senses. Listen to the rustle of trees and leaves, the chirping of birds, the crash of ocean waves...

Nature can re-energize, calm and re-center you and is beneficial for children and adults alike.

Discussions and Adventures to Explore:

1. Ask Questions.
   What is your favorite thing to do outside?
   Where is your favorite outdoor spot?

2. Start a garden!

3. Search for bugs!

4. Collect leaves.

After school Dad came home early to take me to the park. It felt good to be outside on the monkey bars!

I wondered what would happen if an elephant tried to get to the top!!

HA HA HA!

HEE HEE HEE!

Dad and I were laughing and out of breath. My worries seemed far away like the clouds in the sky.

Notes to Adults:

When someone is worried or anxious, they may unconsciously hold tension in their muscles. They may ball their fists, clench their jaw or even tense everything without being aware. You can walk your child through squeezing and releasing the major muscle groups throughout the body.

The tension release technique can lower the heart and breathing rate as it squeezes tension and stress out of the body.

At bedtime, cozy in my jammies and snuggled under the covers, my worry self came back.

Mom came in to help me calm down. "Take a nice deep breath," she said. "Lift your right leg up and point your toes down... then point your toes up. Try the other leg.

Ok, now lift your arms and make a fist. Now shake it out! Try that again. Shrug your shoulders into your neck and squeeze for a count of five.

Now relax. Squeeze your eyes and mouth as if you just took a bite of a sour lemon! Good job relaxing your whole body!"

Notes to Adults:

Be Patient!

You can be a good role model and practice these techniques with your child.

> Keep in mind that each of these techniques are interchangable and can be practiced wherever or whenever they are needed. An example would be practicing gratitude as a bed time routine or at the start of the day. It is what works best for you and your child!

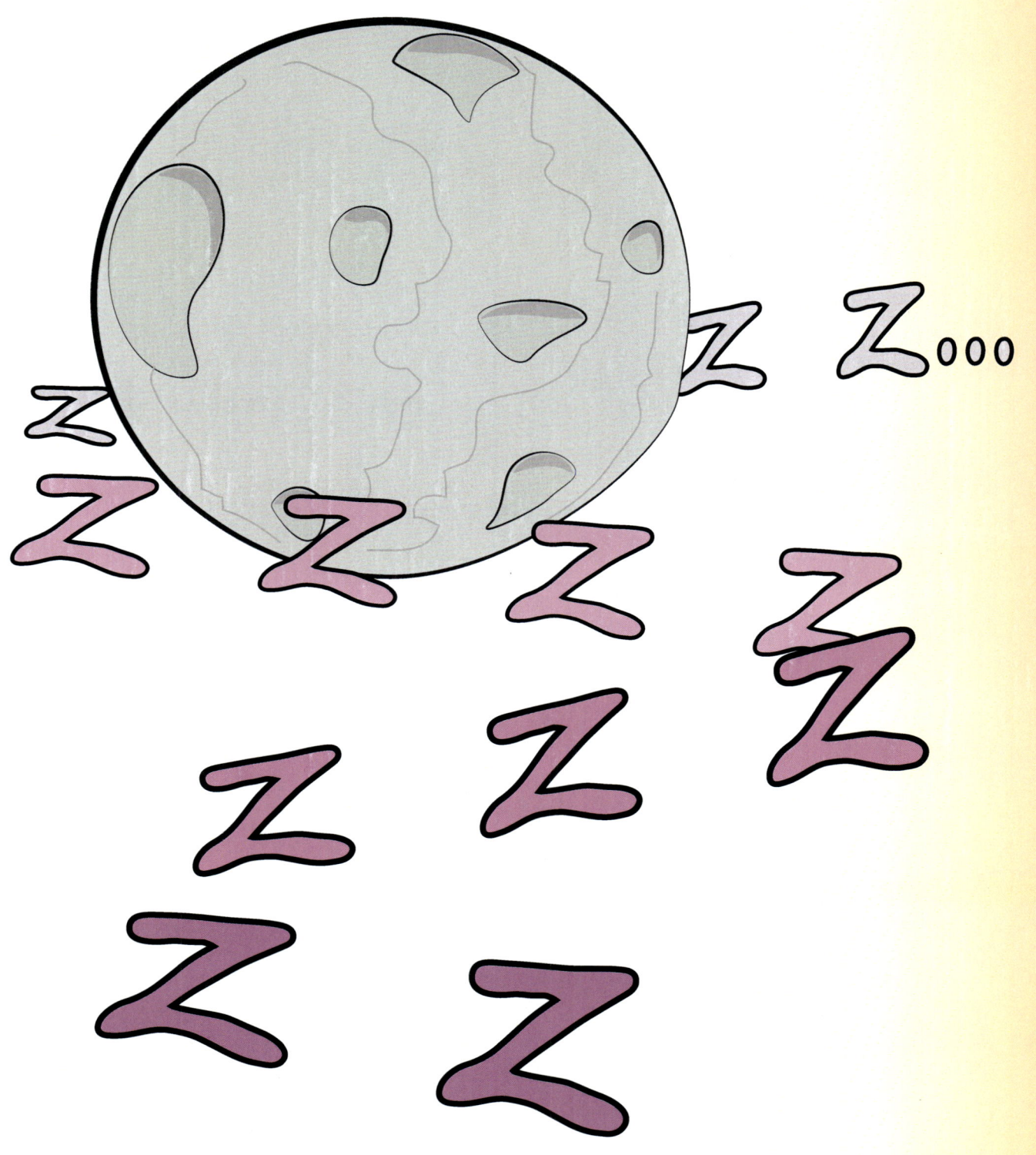

The crickets chirped, the moon was full and James was fast asleep!

The Authors:

Kelly McMahon Brown, MA SAC

Ms. Brown has been working as a New Jersey Certified Student Assistance Counselor for the past 15 years and is currently the President of the New Jersey Association of Student Assistance Professionals. She earned a Master of Arts in Holistic Health Studies from Georgian Court University and is a Certified Child/Adolescent Life Coach. Every day, Kelly helps students cope with school avoidance, substance use/abuse, bullying, anxiety, depression, school motivation, relationship and confidence issues. Ms. Brown uses a holistic approach focusing on the mind, body and spirit.

Arlene Curcio Armbrecht, RN MA

Ms. Armbrecht is a registered nurse with a Masters Degree in Holistic Health. She has over 16 years experience as a certified school nurse within the New Jersey Public School System. Arlene has used her holistic health knowledge in workshops incorporating art, wellness and healing in the school setting, with grief groups and addiction recovery centers. Arlene is the proud mother of three grown children, Kiefer, Meghan and Adam, whom she adores. Ms. Armbrecht believes in the innate power we all have to create happiness and wellness in our lives.

Illustrations:
Arlene Curcio Armbrecht
Adam Curcio Armbrecht

Adam is a freelance artist with a background in graphic design. His expertise was instrumental in the development and enhancement of the book's artwork.

Made in the USA
San Bernardino, CA
21 January 2016